ANDREA V. MILLS

PAMELA M. GALBRAITH

A MAGICAL LIFE

The incredible journey of one woman from small-town nurse to changing the course of mental healthcare for New Mexico.

This book is dedicated to all who shared Pam's magical life.

Cheboygan Crib Light, Pam's favorite Lighthouse

If you met Pam Galbraith, she would invite you into her office and offer you a cup of coffee. And you would begin to talk. There was something about her that made people share. You'd talk about work. Concerns. Maybe something personal. She would listen, comfortable, warm, open. And when you finished your verbal exhale, she would share a story. You'd laugh. And then she'd share her wisdom, somehow connecting people and resources and making a path ahead, in her husky voice, starting with, "Here's what I'd do if I were you."

Stepping into Pam's life is like walking into an elite meeting of superstars. CEOs, presidents, THE Presidents, movers and shakers in the world of healthcare, and government bigwigs all have one story to share: "She was the most amazing mentor, and I wouldn't be where I am if it wasn't for her."

And all she would say is that she'd had a magical life.

CONTENTS

BEGINNINGS

Cheboygan, Michigan, is a small town on the "tip of the mitt." Bisected by the Cheboygan River into east and west, Cheboygan is still a small, intimate community. Green trees, grass and flowers surround the saltbox homes, and water is always in view, from the river to the Straits of Mackinaw.

The Galbraith family moved to Cheboygan via Scottish ancestors who had originally settled in Hamilton, Ontario, Canada. Following the lumber industry, they moved south, crossing the border into the United States.

Rolyn Rutledge Galbraith was born in Cheboygan on September 19, 1904. As an adult, he worked for the Cheboygan Public Works Department, spending 30 years as a grader operator. He was also a member of the volunteer fire department. When he met Marjorie Eileen DuFresne, it was love at first sight.

Rolyn and his grader.

Marjorie was born on October 3, 1908, in Trout Lake, on in the upper peninsula of Michigan. She spent her childhood travelling with her mother, who was a midwife. Marjorie's mother died young, so she became the "mother" for her four rambunctious younger brothers.

Rolyn and Marjorie married in 1947. It was a second marriage for Marjorie, who brought two teenage daughters with her: Rayma, who was 20, and Beth Ann, who was 17.

The newlyweds moved to a small white house with black shutters on Byron Street. Soon Marjorie was pregnant. Pamela Mahala Galbraith was born on the morning of March 6, 1948, at Community Memorial Hospital in Cheboygan, Michigan.

Marjorie was so small up to the date of delivery that many neighbors were surprised when she and Rolyn brought home a strong, healthy 8-pound baby.

Pam was dark haired, bright eyed and full of energy. She thrived within the warmth of her fun and loving family. Rolyn always called her his baby girl, and when she was sick or sad, she would sit in his white leather easy chair with him while he rubbed her ear until she fell asleep. She delighted in the stories he made up each night at bedtime, and his tenderness and gentleness strengthened her and infused her with the compassion she was known for.

Pam and Rolyn.

Marjorie was loving and the disciplinarian in the family. Pam wrote in a journal to her grandchildren that her mom was kind but strict. She taught Pam the importance of hard work and making a difference in the world. She also enforced the idea that a person should always think before speaking, an idea that Pam carried with her throughout her life.

Roaming the lush green streets of her small town along with a pack of neighborhood kids, Pam experienced a joyful childhood. She rode bikes, skated, and swam all over the neighborhood. In the winter, Pam and all of the kids would haul sleds, toboggans, and saucers to various hills around town, or pull-out skates and head to the city ice rink. Pam's home was often the center of the action, being next to an open lot where kids loved to play kick the can and other games.

Pam played the accordion, travelling to fairs and performing.
She also won several awards. She hated playing it,
longing instead to play the harmonica.

Her early elementary school years were spent in Patterson School, a two-room schoolhouse with a play area outside. Even as a child, Pam seemed destined for a life of working hard and helping others. When she was 6, she began getting up at 4 a.m. and helping an arthritic milkman deliver bottles of milk for $1 per day.

Patterson School is still standing.

That hard work continued throughout her school years. Rambunctious and fun-loving, as she moved into junior high, she lettered in cheerleading, football, and basketball. Social and popular, Pam went to Cheboygan High School wearing her dark hair in a bob, with the horn-rimmed glasses, bobby socks and skirts of the time. She always had a way of getting into the middle of the action, whether it was cheering at a game, joining friends at a dance, or building floats in the gym for homecoming. Pam knew everyone by name and was known around school for her big smile and kindness.

Pam's signature horn-rimmed glasses in high school.

Cheboygan High School.

In high school she worked as a car hop at the A&W for 50 cents an hour, plus tips. While there, her sunny disposition and attention to detail won over even the toughest customers. One curmudgeonly regular was known for snapping at servers and for never tipping. Bold as always, Pam took him on while her coworkers avoided him, graciously making sure that his coffee was full and his order was served on time. He still growled but he noticed her efforts, rewarding her with a huge tip one day, a large bag of coins. Pam's boss had her divide it with the entire staff. Rather than being angry about splitting her prize, she peacefully shared. For Pam, helping the old man made it worthwhile. Throughout her life, doing the right thing was her focus and she felt it was its own reward.

DREAMS

Pam graduated from Cheboygan High School in 1966 and planned to follow her childhood dream of becoming a nurse.

Pam wearing her cap and gown in front of her childhood home.

In the 1960s and 1970s, there were three main paths to becoming a nurse. One could go through a three-year program at a local hospital, studying during the day and providing labor to the hospital in 12-hour shifts at night. More expensive but faster was a two-year program for an associate degree of nursing. There was also a four-year bachelor's degree program, but it was costly for students, and hospitals were less eager to hire these graduates because of the higher salary required by them.

Pam chose a three-year hospital nursing program at the Saginaw General Hospital School of Nursing. She was secretly terrified to move three hours away from her family and friends but shared her fear only with her journal. Her family couldn't afford to pay for her training, so she worked several jobs and lived with roommates to make ends meet.

The nursing program ran on a traditional school schedule, leaving summers free. Pam went home each summer and Christmas, earning money for the next semester by working at Carnation Restaurant, a family-style eatery in Cheboygan. The owners required staff to take orders by memory. Pam had a tremendous ability to retain information and enjoyed the challenge. On her free evenings, she would go to Deed's, a local bar, enjoying beers with friends and family.

Pam passionately savored every moment. She was devoted to her family and friends, and staying close to everyone in Cheboygan suited her perfectly. She soon became engaged to an old high school boyfriend, David Connor. It seemed that Pam's sunny life would never see a day of rain. She was 19 and in love, pursuing her dream job and close as ever with her family. Then tragedy struck. In January of 1968 her dad suddenly died from a heart attack, leaving 19-year-old Pam without his gentle, loving support. Shortly after that, David was drafted and sent to Vietnam where he was killed in action.

Rolyn and Marjorie.

Losing her father and fiancé in one year changed her. She wrote in a journal, "When someone you love dies ... a little piece of your heart goes with them and leaves a space." Full of grief, Pam dealt with her pain with a new laser focus on her studies. She changed nursing programs, enrolling in a newly formed two-year associate's program through Saginaw School of Nursing at North Central Michigan College in Petoskey, just an hour from Cheboygan.

Pam continued to work several minimum wage jobs to put herself through school. Later on, she said she ate so much peanut butter, she never wanted to eat it again. Having three roommates helped make ends meet, and as they were all friends, they creatively helped one another by making meals. One roommate's unforgettable fondue lived on in Pam's memory forever. Grateful to come home after a long day and have a tasty meal waiting, Pam dug in. When she was done eating, Pam asked what the meat was, having not recognized the flavor. Sheepishly the roommate admitted that, being short on cash, he had caught and cooked one of the neighborhood squirrels.

Pam with a group of college friends.
She had an extraordinary ability to make and keep friends,
staying in touch throughout her entire life.

While in college, Pam began driving back to Cheboygan on weekends to work at Community Memorial Hospital as a nursing assistant and ward clerk for a 30-bed acute medical unit. She took care of clerical tasks and patient care services that didn't require a license.

NURSING

In the 1970s nurses still wore starched, white uniforms, complete with white oxford shoes and white hose. The trademark tidy, folded caps were a badge of honor for nurses, won after a challenging period of training and studies, and given at a capping ceremony that was a rite of passage. The cap represented dignity, dedication, and pride in service, and sat on the hair, carefully pinned in place.

Wearing her crisp white uniform, hair in a bob, horn-rimmed glasses framing her bright eyes, Pam graduated with her associate's in nursing in 1970. Marjorie watched Pam receive her white cap and pin, tears in her eyes. She was the first Galbraith woman to receive any education past high school.

After graduation, Pam moved back to Cheboygan and began working full-time at Community Memorial Hospital. She had a new roommate, Linda Nichols, who was slightly older and also worked at the hospital. Pam and Linda moved into a small, yellow, flat-roofed two-bedroom cottage off the point in the Straits of Mackinac. As a housewarming gift, a friend gave her a cat named "Damnit." She settled in, glad to be near her mom and her childhood friends.

Pam and Marjorie at her graduation

The "Mighty Mac" opened in 1957.
Pam loved the bridge, having watched it being built.

Quickly rising to the position of nursing supervisor, responsible for the entire 150-bed hospital, Pam wrote in a journal that she felt inadequately prepared for the job. She journaled that the nursing educational programs had not prepared her emotionally or technically to do the job. She confessed to her journal that she tended to be very independent and headstrong, but desperately needed the experience and patience of her seasoned co-workers. She wanted a mentor, and she sought them out, spending her days asking questions and shadowing the experienced nurses around her. Understanding the need for mentorship became a foundational idea for Pam that stayed with her, becoming a hallmark of her approach to work.

In the early years of her career, Pam picked up smoking, a habit that she was known for throughout her life. In the 1970s, smoking was seen as a relaxing, social activity, akin to joining co-workers for a cup of coffee or a beer. Nurses enjoyed relaxing with a cigarette at the nurse's station while making up reports and talking about patients. It was also seen as a part of patient care, and nurses would often smoke with them. As someone who relished spending time with everyone, Pam found the habit relaxing and useful.

Six months after beginning her full-time career as a nurse, Pam was offered a charge-nurse position. In a journal, Pam wrote that she realized that she wanted to be more involved in decisions affecting her work, so she gave an enthusiastic "yes" to the position.

Cheboygan Memorial hospital in the 1950s–1960s.

This new position was a minimal exposure to management but exciting to a powerhouse of energy like Pam. She loved it and was eager to experience more. Six months after accepting that position, Pam was promoted to an evening supervisor role with even more responsibility. This advancement meant that Pam was the only administrative agent in the 150-bed hospital during her shift. She had to work as a liaison between all hospital departments at night, negotiating resources and need. She was also required to determine the appropriate staffing needs of each nursing department of the hospital, based on patient requirements and available medical and financial resources.

Pam excelled at understanding and managing both budgets and staff resources. She also learned to identify and investigate problems with staff and other personnel, journaling that it forced her to learn to recognize the difference between non-problems and symptoms versus major issues.

LEAVINGS

Pam loved being home but was feeling a pull to leave. The deaths of her dad and fiancé still were an emotional hardship for her and she journaled that every day she spent in Cheboygan reminded her of them. She was devoted to her family and childhood experiences so much so that she and Linda even rented the home Pam had grown up in. Unfortunately, this made it even harder to get over the death of Rolyn. Added stress with other members of her family began to convince her that it was time to leave the town she loved.

During her time off, Pam continued to hang out at Deeds, the local bar that she had frequented since her late teens. There she met Annie McClain, a bartender. Annie's family owned a chain of popular grocery stores in the upper peninsula of Michigan, but she had no desire to go into the grocery business. As they talked in the evenings, they realized that they both longed to experience something outside of Cheboygan. Their thirst for something new, maybe even something out west, grew.

Marjorie, who valued her daughter's need for independence and purpose, encouraged her to pursue this new adventure. Pam could see that her mom wasn't in good health, but
Marjorie reminded Pam that there were plenty of other family
members, including her two older daughters, in Cheboygan to
care for her. Pam decided to go.

Twenty-four-year-old Pam had spent two years nursing
full-time in Cheboygan and had gained hundreds of hours of
mentorship and experience. In April 1972, while Michigan
was still chilly and full of slush, she and Annie, each with a
new '72 Volkswagen Beetle, packed up everything they owned,
including Damnit. They had enough cash to drive across the
country, and planned to head south to I-40, and then west.

On her final night in Cheboygan, Pam held a going away
party at Deeds. She and her friends laughed, told stories and
shared memories over beers, a haze of cigarette smoke filling
the air. Halfway into the night, Pam's mom came to spend
some precious hours with her youngest daughter, which earned
Marjorie the nickname "Crasher Mom."

Pam put Cheboygan in her rear-view mirror and headed
out of town the next morning. Michigan was still icy, but once
she crossed the Mississippi River, the countryside warmed up
and flattened out. Pam and Annie didn't have extra money and
didn't take time for sightseeing, other than roadside stops.

Pam and her packed VW Bug leaving Michigan.

About a week later they drove into New Mexico, the Land of Enchantment. Looming in the distance was a mountain. Over the hours of driving, it rose up and spread in rippling waves of green. Soft white clouds filled the skies, rain showers showed along the horizon, and the smell of sage filled the cars though the open windows. The Land of Enchantment began to work its magic. Pam and Annie left the highway in Albuquerque and drove down historic Route 66, looking for a motel appropriate for two young women and their cats. They chose a small, inexpensive one, unpacked and went to bed.

Pam and Annie hadn't planned to settle in New Mexico, but they were nearly out of money. Albuquerque had a population of about 300,000 people, a military base and several hospitals. It was hundreds of miles to the next comparable city. Pam had arrived in the city she would call home for the rest of her life. Some locals jokingly call New Mexico the Land of Entrapment, but more likely it was the magic that Pam felt infused her life that had brought her.

Both women headed out after breakfast the next morning to find jobs. Annie went to local lounges and bars to find a job as a bartender while Pam headed to the hospitals to find a job as a nurse. Route 66 had three major hospitals along it. The largest hospital in the state, Presbyterian, was nearby and Pam applied there first. Nurses were desperately needed in Albuquerque, and she was immediately hired to work in the emergency department.

CHANGES

Heading back to the hotel, Pam thought she was settled now that she had a job. Just as a small pebble dropped in water can cause ripples of change, Pam was about to encounter a moment in time that would ripple and change her entire life. While working her first day in the ER at Presbyterian, a heart attack patient came in. Pam worked hard with a team to stabilize him. Once he was stable, the hospital staff looked up his insurance and saw that he was uninsured. Only one hospital in Albuquerque served uninsured patients at that time. As per hospital policy, they put the man in an ambulance to go up the road to Bernalillo County Medical Center (BCMC, now University of New Mexico Hospital). Horrified that an acute patient would be sent away in poor condition just because of an inability to pay, Pam angrily jumped into the ambulance and traveled with him, working to make sure he remained stable.

Pam was so dismayed by the hospital's policy, that with only one day of work logged at Presbyterian, she never returned. Instead she applied to be a nurse at BCMC. As someone who always put doing the right thing ahead of anything else, she was not willing to work for a hospital that put money ahead of need. She was immediately hired as a staff nurse in the Medical Intensive Care Unit.

Magically, Pam had come to the exact place she would work for the next 33 years. She would become known as the "matron of medicine," leaving a legacy that would impact the entire state of New Mexico. At the time, though, she only knew that BCMC had a mission and commission to serve those who had no other resources. Pam had been taught by Rolyn and Marjorie that all people deserve the same respect and care, and she had already been focused on this in her life, from the arthritic milkman to the old man at the A&W and on through her adulthood. Pam now had the opportunity to serve thousands of people with that level of respect and care.

HEARTACHE

BCMC had opened in 1954 as the Bernalillo County Indian Hospital and was meant to serve the Native American population in New Mexico, maintaining at least 100 beds for them. It also served the growing city of Albuquerque, the largest in the state.

BCMC from a 1950 postcard.
When Pam began working at the hospital, it looked the same.

When the UNM School of Medicine was founded in 1964, the hospital, directly across the street, became the primary teaching facility for the university. The hospital was renamed Bernalillo County Medical Center in 1968 to show that it was a hospital for the entire community. In 1969, the university took over operations of the hospital.

UNM had been running BCMC for three years when Pam began working there. The hospital was small but growing, with a few hundred employees. Albuquerque, with two major interstates meeting in the middle of town and connecting the United States from north to south and east to west, also had a booming military base and two governmental labs. It was rapidly growing and Pam arrived, as if by magic, at just the right time.

1972 was already a banner year for Pam for life change, but it sadly also brought Pam more heartache. Her mom grew sick while on a Christmas trip to visit San Antonio family. Pam was able to rush home from work and fly to her in Texas. As soon as she saw her mom, she knew she didn't have long left. Pam immediately got her on a plane and back to Cheboygan. At Community General Hospital, a few days later, Marjorie died of heart disease. Pam and her sisters buried their mom in Cheboygan next to Rolyn.

Despite being nearly two decades younger, Pam was the leader among her siblings, and it was her job to read the will and divide the estate. Full of grief, Pam returned to Albuquerque, where she threw herself into work to help manage her heartache.

Pam in 1972.

Working in New Mexico, a desert state that had one of the highest rates of poverty in the country, was a shocking experience for Pam. Diseases that were largely unseen in the rest of the country – like the plague, rabies, and the unpredictable hantavirus – were common in impoverished rural areas. They were so problematic that in the '60s, UNM Medical School gave new students T-shirts emblazoned with "Land of the Flea and Home of the Plague."

New Mexico is the fifth-largest state in the union by area. Its poverty combined with much of the population's extreme distances from cities and hospitals created other problems. Patients from rural areas and tribal reservations would often avoid going to the hospital, often due to a lack of resources needed to drive the hundreds of miles to the hospital. Frequently, many of these patients arrived too late for treatment to be effective.

Healthcare in New Mexico was challenging and difficult, and very different from the health landscape of her hometown. Rather than scaring Pam, it energized her. Missing family, but loving this unique new home, Pam wrote in her journal that she knew Rolyn and Marjorie were watching her from heaven. And from heaven they would have seen a young woman who was blossoming into a force that would impact the entire state of New Mexico.

Pam stayed connected with friends from Cheboygan and constantly updated her collection of albums with their photos, birthday cards, special letters, and notes. She also added photos and notes about certain patients whose stories impacted her the most. One photo was of a 10-year-old girl named Maria* (name changed for privacy).

Maria was brought to BCMC by a family member one hot summer day. She was severely ill from hepatitis. This highly contagious virus was common on the reservations and hard to treat. Pam had been trained to treat hepatitis, but this was her first hands-on experience with it. As she spent weeks caring for Maria, she noticed no one came to visit the young girl, so she sat with her, talking, telling stories, and hearing about her life. Daily, after these conversations, Pam would take detailed notes about her case.

Maria's treatment seemed to work, and she was released from the hospital. Her family decided to leave her in Albuquerque and released her from their care. Pam was now fully invested in her life, so she brought Maria back her small apartment and planned to adopt her. Before she was able to do so, Maria relapsed and died.

Her death shook Pam, then 27, to her core, and her story became a cornerstone of Pam's approach to medical care, highlighting the need for more accessible rural healthcare. Maria's death also was behind her constant drive to pursue better outcomes and equal care for all, regardless of income level or location.

5 WEST

Pam began her work at BCMC as a staff nurse in the Medical Intensive Care Unit. By her second year, she became an instructor for staff development.

Three years later, in 1975 Pam was promoted to head nurse on a medical floor called 5 West. Five West was a 42-bed acute medical unit. Her new responsibilities included preparing budgets, dealing with administrative tasks, making sure there was appropriate staffing for each shift, counseling and disciplining employees while maintaining quality and client satisfaction. It was a big role to fill but familiar to Pam, who had completed similar duties at the 150-bed hospital in Cheboygan.

Pam had always loved being in the center of the action, and she thrived under the pressure and pace required for her as head nurse. She was known to have a metaphorical finger on the pulse of every person in her unit, from patients and their families to nurses and doctors. One friend commented that she even had the rare skill of excelling as a liaison between patients and doctors. She was in her element and shone.

While Pam loved its vision and mission, in truth BCMC in the 1970s was just a small hospital with a poor reputation in the area. Locals referred to it as the "county hospital" and it was often the last choice for medical care for the area. There was room to change the local opinion of the hospital and Pam wanted to help make it happen. With her characteristic energy, she volunteered to help in the growing medical school at UNM, teaching class units like "Nursing Care of the Adult Leukemia Patient" and "Introduction to the Patient." She also opened 5 West up to nursing students for study and observation. She regularly organized and ran first-aid tents at major New Mexico events like the State Fair and Balloon Fiesta to raise awareness about the services offered by BCMC. She knew that this volunteer work would go a long way toward good will in the community.

The hospital needed to go beyond image and change its internal workings. To help, Pam joined a team of nurses working on improving training for her peers. The program she helped create had two tiers. The first was for new nurses. She recognized that keeping a static requirement of classes and training for every new nurse on-boarding was unnecessary. The team created a new program that looked at the training and proficiencies each nurse brought, personalizing the training to fit the nurse. Zealous in improving patient care, her team also made additional skill training more accessible to the nurses by moving classes into the hospital and providing more convenient course offering times.

Pam received personal commendation for her work on the team in the form of letters from her superiors and hospital administrators, keeping them in her personal albums at home. Her supervisors asked her to help reorganize current systems in the outpatient department. When she finished, they asked her to do the same work in other departments. Seemingly by magic, everything that came into her hands ended up running more efficiently and smoothly.

From that one magical pebble she dropped by changing hospitals on her first day of work, Pam's professional life was expanding like ripples in a pond. Now her personal life was about to expand as well. Since the death of her fiancé eight years earlier, she hadn't been interested in dating. That was about to change.

LOVE

When Jerry Vigil walked into the Apollo Lounge in the San Mateo Lanes, a bowling alley and bar in Albuquerque, he was just stopping in after work to see the manager, a good friend of his. In a suit, he stood out from the typical blue-jeans-and-T-shirt-wearing locals. Weaving his way through the lounge, he noticed a woman in a white nurse's uniform at the bar, head down. She wasn't drinking, she was just sitting. Intrigued, he said hello, and asked if he could help.

Pam had been crying and wiped her tears away. She looked up, her dark eyes bright and sharp behind horn-rimmed glasses, and invited Jerry to sit down with her. Voice husky with tears, she began to talk about a child she had treated that day. Like Maria, she had come in from the reservation with hepatitis. Pam and the other nursing staff of 5 West did their best to help her, but the parents had waited too long to make the long trip to Albuquerque, and she died. Angry, the family accused Pam and the hospital staff of not doing enough to save their daughter. As head nurse, Pam felt a burden of responsibility for the outcome.

Pam talked and Jerry listened. Pleased with his company, she introduced him to her friend Annie, who was a bartender for the lounge.

Jerry asked Pam for her number and a few days later called and invited her to take a tour of Albuquerque with him. Jerry's family, the Vigils, had been in New Mexico for generations. His history lesson and tour were dynamic and fun. Like Pam, Jerry had grown up in a small town where he knew everyone. And like Pam, he had moved to a bigger city for more opportunities. She told him about the small town of Cheboygan she had grown up in, the Great Lakes, the green forests, the long winters, and the people. Jerry told her about his boyhood in Clayton, a town in northeastern New Mexico, and about the history of the Vigil family. They talked for hours.

From that first date, Jerry kept calling with invitations and Pam kept saying yes. After a few dates she confessed to Jerry she had never been dated anyone who wore a suit like him. Cheboygan was a factory town and business attire was rarely seen. Albuquerque was a small, western town with a mix of casual styles. Jerry, who was an agency manager for Modern Woodman of America, wore a suit as part of his job. Pam liked it.

It was late in 1976 when 28-year-old Pam began dating Jerry. She knew that he was newly divorced with two young daughters. Jerry kept his relationship with Pam private and didn't discuss it – not even with his daughters. His daughters were living with their mother, which made it easy to keep the relationship private.

Even as they dated, Pam maintained her independence, going on trips with friends from work, keeping her night schedule because she liked it best, and spending evenings at Mama Mia's with co-workers drinking beer and discussing work. Jerry didn't mind her independence, and instead admired it. After several months, he asked her to marry him, and Pam, who had been alone for years, said yes.

While New Mexico was becoming home, Michigan held Pam's heart and was where she wanted to get married, close to her lifelong friends and family.

On September 10, 1977, Pam and Jerry were married at St. Paul's United Methodist Church in Cheboygan, the same small church where Pam had been baptized and confirmed. Floor-to-ceiling windows opening up in the front of the church sanctuary brought the dense Michigan forest close. Pam's yellow, oriental-styled dress dazzled against the background of trees. Her sister Beth was her matron of honor and her brother-in-law Paul was Jerry's best man. Because her dad had died, her nephew, also named Paul, gave her away. Jerry's mom, Ione, flew in from New Mexico. Surrounded by childhood friends and family, Pam was married. Proud of her Scottish heritage and well-established in her career and community, Pam chose to keep her maiden name of Galbraith.

Pam, Jerry, and Jerry's mother, Ione, at their wedding.

Finances were tight for the newlyweds who had already traveled far for the wedding, so they stayed near Cheboygan, driving up the coast to nearby Mackinaw City for the night. Pam had forgotten to bring any other shoes on their honeymoon and thought she looked silly wearing jeans with yellow high heels. Giggling, she and Jerry went to a store, grabbed flip flops off the store shelf, and headed off to enjoy their brief vacation.

After their honeymoon, Jerry brought Pam home to his small stucco house in the North Valley area of Albuquerque. He had had the home cleaned, but the house felt empty and unloved. Jerry's ex-wife had taken almost everything with her.

Pam worked with their small budget to make it feel more homelike.

A month after they were married, Jerry's 9-year-old daughter, Jacqueline, decided to live with them full time. Her little sister, Jennifer, was 3 and lived with their mom, Jane, staying with Pam and Jerry on weekends and holidays. Pam's decorating efforts began in the girls' rooms, where she cut out felt butterflies for the white curtains and put blue and red bedspreads on the beds.

Despite her efforts to create a home in the space, Pam constantly felt uncomfortable staying in a house that Jerry had lived in during an unhappy marriage. Finally, she confessed to Jerry that she was struggling to feel like she belonged there. Jerry understood, and they purchased a different home that would be all theirs.

Jerry was determined to have a peaceful marriage after his previous relationship was fraught with difficulty. He was able to maintain peace to some degree by recognizing Pam's leadership. Jacqueline recalled that Pam was assertive and ready to take charge. She always dealt directly with problems but also worked hard to be kind. As the family adjusted, Pam, like her mother, became the disciplinarian in the home. Jerry was always more tender and available, like Pam's dad.

Full of fun and laughter, Pam often joked that she only made toast and reservations, and since she didn't cook, nearly every dinner was eaten in a restaurant, something new for the girls who had rarely eaten out before. Pam loved simple food, so they ate at family restaurants like IHOP®, Furr's Cafeteria, and Village Inn. At home the most cooking she did was tossing a tortilla in the microwave. She still smoked but took her Tareyton cigarettes outside, no matter the weather.

Pam and Jerry a few years after their marriage.

As they built a new life together, Pam carved out the weekends for family fun. Jerry had joined a fast-pitch softball team and Pam and the girls attended every game on the weekends, cheering him on. Jerry also loved golf, and Pam attended his tournaments, though she never played. Adding to weekend fun was a pool Jerry had installed for her after they moved to their new home. Michigan girl through and through, Pam loved the desert but *needed* her water.

GROWTH

Maureen Boshier first met Pam when she was working as head nurse in 5 West. Maureen's friend, Ursula Manfretti, was constantly in 5 West to visit her husband, who was being treated for leukemia. In the 1970s, oncology was not in a separate medical unit. The BCMC Cancer Center was established in 1975, but in the hospital, cancer patients and other specialty patients, were admitted to an acute medical floor for treatment.

Cancer treatments were just becoming more common, and chemotherapy was administered by nurses. Based on the diagnosis, a doctor would assign the appropriate drug and dosage. The nurses would then prepare an IV drip, add the prescribed amount of medication and treat the patient. Pam was one of just a handful of nurses at BCMC trained to prepare chemotherapy and other cancer treatments.

Maureen, who worked for the National Institute of Health at that time, visited the Manfretti family almost daily. As she watched Pam work, she noticed that Pam was in tune with everyone on her floor. "She was an exceptional nurse about patient care and the science of nursing. She was extremely compassionate but didn't sugarcoat things," Maureen recalled.

Maureen wasn't the only person who noticed her tremendous abilities. Her supervisors all gave her accolades for her exceptional work, and an album of letters and notes that she kept from the hospital grew. She was told by the director of nursing, Helen Kee, that she was uniquely gifted. Helen encouraged her to consider working in administration. Pam loved patient care and said no.

Pam may not have been ready to consider an administrative role, but her leadership couldn't overlook her organizational and administrative abilities. When the hospital planned to open a 12-bed semi-intensive care unit, Pam was put in charge of preparations. She created the budget, oversaw the renovations and protocols for the unit, and she made critical decisions on staffing, supplies, policies, and procedures. She did such an excellent job that for two years she worked as department head for both 5 West and the new unit.

In 1976, Pam was asked by the hospital administration to spend three months as clinic supervisor. This meant that she would be responsible for managing all the details of 40 clinics, including staffing, budgets and patient care. It was a huge step out of her comfort zone, but she agreed to do it – with the caveat that she would be allowed to return to her job as head nurse. In three months, she implemented a new billing structure, adjusted the staff, and streamlined the operations to allow for more satisfied patients receiving a higher quality of care at a lower cost to both the hospital and patient.

That move was the catalyst that shifted something in her personal vision. Pam had consistently shied away from the idea of stepping into administrative work because it would remove her from hands-on patient care. While running the clinics, she had realized that administrative work would give her a greater ability to make changes that improved the care and outcome of patients.

One of Pam's greatest strengths came from her love of stories and knowing the right moment to lighten the mood with humor. Pam collected stories about funny things that happened to her. One favorite was about a man who complained that he couldn't rest because of all the sheep running in and out of his room. After visiting him several times, she finally promised to keep the nonexistent sheep in the hall. They wouldn't bother him any longer.

Another work story came from several people suffering from botulism. These patients were transported to 5 West and BCMC from a town three hours away. The culprit had been a three-bean salad. One man gradually became paralyzed from the disease until he was unable to move or speak.

Eager to help him and keep him comfortable, everyone including his wife began to shout as they spoke to him, hoping that he heard them. With treatment, his body began to relax and he eventually was able to move one toe. Finally, he could blink. Excited to communicate with him, Pam asked him to blink out letters of the alphabet to spell words. He managed to spell out, "I'm paralyzed, not deaf." Pam and the others adjusted their volume accordingly.

Pam was always quick to see the funny side of things, but she was also able to see the need and the way to help it. The botulism incident went beyond a funny story. It spurred Pam to create a program for special training in the care of botulism victims. With it, she created a specialty team unlike any other in New Mexico at that time.

In 1978, an opportunity opened for her to become the assistant director of nursing for her division. Helen Kee, the director of nursing for the hospital, encouraged Pam to apply. She got the promotion and with it her first exposure to a whole new level of administration, or as she called it, the "macro-operations" of the hospital. She loved it.

It might have been chance, or maybe it was the magic that Pam felt permeated her life, but two months after her promotion to assistant director of nursing, Helen stepped down. The hospital administration asked Pam to take her position and work as acting director of nursing. This meant that she was responsible for more than 400 staff members and had to manage an annual budget of over $9 million . Her employee reviews show that she was outstanding in her quality of work, quantity of work, and dependability.

Pam was capable but humbly aware of her shortcomings. She was petrified in her new role, having been thrown in with very little training and no mentor to guide her. Every night she came home and told Jerry that she was afraid she was making terrible mistakes.

A large part of Pam's fear stemmed from what she felt was a lack of education. She only had an associate's degree for nursing (ADN), which meant that she was technically under-qualified for the job. In her core, Pam still saw herself as the small-town woman from Cheboygan.

Bill Johnson, the CEO for the hospital, may have added stress as well. He was a former military officer who had retired in New Mexico. He was a controversial and difficult leader. His military career made him unforgiving of mistakes. To the surprise of many who knew him, he gave Pam time and patience, commending her work in several formal memos for her employee file.

With his support and Jerry's encouragement, Pam slowly got her feet under her. She was an intuitive problem solver, a genius with budgets, and gifted with not only making people like her but with getting them to work together. Her departments began to run more smoothly, resulting in improved patient care and reviews. One letter from a hospital administrator stated, "During the past eight months, your performance as acting director of nursing has been outstanding. Your drive, confidence and good humor kept the nursing department going through some very rocky times."

Whether it was magic or a lack of experienced nurses in the sparsely populated Southwest, no one could be found to fill the Director of Nursing role, so Pam kept what was meant to be a temporary position for several years.

Pam and then-Mayor Kinney.

BCMC was officially renamed University of New Mexico Hospital in 1979, showcasing the close relationship between the two institutions. Part of that relationship was a generous plan to help employees desiring to get more education. Pam thought it was the perfect opportunity to fill in her educational gaps.

EDUCATION

The University of New Mexico didn't have the required programs for business available at that time, so in 1980 Pam applied to a Certificate in Advanced Education Leadership, CAEL, program for 45 credit hours in business administration. She additionally applied to the University of Albuquerque, a small Catholic liberal arts college that offered a Bachelor of Science in Health Care Administration.

In a letter included with her application to the University of Albuquerque, Bill wrote: "I would like to comment that Ms. Galbraith is one of the most talented managers I have ever worked with in 25 years of healthcare...".

Pursuing her management degree seemed to give Pam a boost of confidence. She began to recognize her own gifts and abilities, as well as see how much experience she had gained during her years of nursing.

As she began to pursue higher education, more doors magically began to open. In 1981, Carrie Tingley Hospital – originally founded in the small town of Truth or Consequences, New Mexico, to serve children with disabilities – merged with

UNM Hospital to serve as a children's hospital for the entire state. Because Albuquerque was near the middle of the huge desert state, the plan was to physically house Carrie Tingley in the UNM Hospital building, making it more accessible to everyone. Pam was asked to work as a liaison between UNM Hospital and Carrie Tingley Hospital, facilitating the contracts between the two organizations. Her work on the merger earned her more accolades from the administrators of both hospitals.

MONEY

Steve McKernan joined UNM Hospital as an accounting manager in 1980. Eventually he would be promoted to controller in 1982, continue to rise to CFO in 1986, and finally work as CEO from 1996-2017. But in 1980, he was working in the financial office for a hospital that was losing money and had significant debt. With high rates of uninsured and changing rules for payments from Medicaid, Medicare, and Indian Health Services, as well as consistently delayed payments, the hospital struggled to make ends meet. It was doing so poorly that it was borrowing to meet bi-weekly payrolls. Part of Steve's job was to work on getting it out of the red.

As head nurse, Pam was required to meet with the accounting and administration department heads for weekly budget meetings. The meetings were often volatile as they showed needs and decided how to spread their sparse financial resources out so that they covered medications, treatments, and salaries, as well as building maintenance and other details.

In the summer of 1981, Steve and others created a plan to get the hospital out of debt. Their plan placed the hospital under tremendous financial constraints. Pam, as acting director of nursing met with Steve weekly. Steve and Pam frequently butted heads in their varied approaches to making the money stretch.

A year into his job, Steve was preparing to get married and take time off for a honeymoon. He and Pam had left a meeting in tense disagreement. Steve recalled: "I was working in my office later that day when I noticed someone standing in front of me. It was Pam with a basket with wine and cheese and crackers. I said, 'Hi, Pam,' not knowing what to expect. She replied, 'I know you and I don't agree on everything,' and handed him the basket. 'You're about to get married. The next four to five days will be crazy. My suggestion is for you to take this basket and take Becky off to a quiet place while everyone else is going nuts. Take time to dedicate yourselves to each other and have a great marriage.' We had been arguing over money and budgets, but she was thoughtful enough to get the basket and prioritize Becky and I having a good marriage. Whenever I got upset at Pam, I would remember those thoughtful things."

Pam's ability to separate work from relationships was one of her greatest strengths. While she was willing to aggressively protect her people and do whatever it took for the greater good, she could easily put tension from work aside. She was actively thoughtful, giving notes and cards to recognize great work, and giving gifts for birthdays, weddings, and new babies.

Pam and Steve McKernan.

As the hospital worked to climb out of debt, employees were asked to help with the mill levy campaigns. Mill levies made up 25 percent of the hospital budget. They were also a vital part of a contract between UNM Hospital and the state of New Mexico, which leased the hospital the land it was on. To maintain its lease, the state required UNM Hospital to pass a mill levy every eight years and to keep 100 beds for Native American patients.

The first year that Pam worked on the mill levy, she mobilized the workforce as a grassroots program with administration and staff in matching T-shirts going house to house, putting signs on doors. Pam felt that employees in T-shirts advocating personally was vital to passing mill levies with community support. It worked and each mill levy passed, keeping the hospital open.

10 MAGICAL YEARS

In April 1982, Pam celebrated her 10-year anniversary at BCMC/UNM Hospital. UNM Hospital was growing from a tiny, financially strapped county facility to a medical center with a high reputation locally and nationally. In the 10 years Pam had worked at the hospital, it had grown from a few hundred employees to more than one thousand. The number of beds had doubled to 300. Most importantly, the financial programs had succeeded so well that the hospital was out of debt.

Medicine had changed dramatically since Pam entered nursing, and hospitals were adjusting to new technologies and standards. Trauma ratings, though voluntary, were a helpful new addition to medicine, allowing hospitals to showcase the level of care they offered. The White House used hospital trauma ratings as it charted paths for flying the president across the country, choosing routes near those that were rated at the highest level.

UNM Hospital had achieved the Level 1 Trauma Center standard in 1983. As the only Level 1 Trauma center in New Mexico, it was now nationally important as a lead hospital in the southwestern path of presidential flyovers. Each time a president traveled, an entire area of the hospital was set aside. An advance team would come from the White House to make sure the hospital was set up the way it needed to be should the president have a health emergency. Pam was often the liaison for these teams, and some of Pam's most treasured letters are from the White House under presidents George W. Bush and Bill Clinton, thanking her for her service.

By the 1980s, trauma rankings required specific protocols and training, so with her amazing attention to detail, Pam was asked to help develop them at UNM Hospital. She organized the nurse and tech staffs, having each department prepare special protocols to combine with training and accreditation necessary for the hospital to gain and maintain its Level 1 Trauma rating.

The training required unity in the staff, which was difficult to create because of competition between different departments. Pam was able to cut through the competition. "Pam had a remarkable ability to get everyone in a room focused on a goal," Steve recalled. "If they were going berserk, she could get them on task and on goal."

Lifeguard Air Emergency Services was an important piece of UNM Hospital's trauma ranking. The program brought the first air medical flight program to New Mexico, vital in a state with hundreds of miles between cities and hospitals and double the national average of trauma patients. One program Pam oversaw was the Lifeguard helicopter program.

In the winter of 1985, shortly after the program started, a Lifeguard helicopter crashed in the mountains outside of Taos on the way to pick up a cardiac patient. The pilot and two flight nurses aboard died. The tragedy shook the hospital staff, as well as communities of New Mexico. Pam, grieving with her employees, organized a memorial event for the families and the hospital.

Pam with an early Lifeguard team.

Pam was now 34, married with two stepdaughters, and had total responsibility for the operation of the entire inpatient nursing division comprised of 18 separate departments.

She was able to complete her Bachelor of Science in Healthcare Administration at the University of Albuquerque in 1984. From there she applied to the newly formed University of Phoenix for a Master of Business Administration. The University of Phoenix allowed a flexible schedule with night classes that were more accessible for working students. Pam joined a group of students that included her friend Maureen.

A "self-report" created for her master's program application showed that she was overqualified for many of the programs she was applying for. She had to petition for credit hours based on experience, because her areas of responsibility grew faster than her ability to complete a degree. In her petition to the university, she asked for work experience-based credits for classes such as Business Administration (she had been lead administrator for 18 departments), Introduction to Data Processing (she was working as liaison for the installation of a state-of-the art computer system), Principles of Accounting (she was managing a multi-million-dollar budget yearly), and Organizational Dynamics (she had already reorganized several clinics and the entire educational system in place for nurses). The self-report included letters from Bill as well as department heads of other areas touting her experience and petitioning for credit hours on her behalf. She received them.

Amy Boule, Maureen Boshier, and Pam.

Jacqueline and Jennifer reflected on that time, remembering that "she was a major multitasker and could do everything at once. And she was never stressed out." For Pam, "relaxing" meant sitting on the sofa, working on her college courses while watching "Law & Order" or helping the girls with their homework.

With so much to do, she saved time where she could, including in the way she drove. She was a renowned speeder, racking up tickets, especially on her way to and from work. She always paid them, but there was a greater price. Pam and Jerry used a post office box, and one evening after work when she picked up the mail, she saw a letter from the state of New Mexico. Startled, she told the person next to her, "Oh no! They've cancelled my license!"

Pam was ordered to driving school to get her license reinstated. Mistakenly, she was placed in a class for people who had driven while under the influence. When she realized what was happening, she told the teacher, "I don't drink and drive! I speed and drive!" She was invited to stay in the class because they would get a free lunch. She did ... and every student got food poisoning from the food. Having completed the class, Pam got her license back – and she continued to speed.

DOWNSTAIRS

When she completed her bachelor's degree, Bill invited Pam to come "downstairs" to full-time administration. "Downstairs" was comprised of a nearly all-male staff, including many ex-military officers who had been stationed at the Air Force base in Albuquerque, retired and stayed for the beautiful landscapes and fantastic weather. Because Albuquerque was still a relatively small city, the hospital was one of the few places with high-level administrative needs. Many of the men found it difficult to put aside their ideas of military culture, so the work culture in administration was harsh and regimented.

She and others jokingly called the administrative offices "mahogany row." Although she now had more education and had consistently performed exceptionally well, she was anxious, fearful that she didn't have the necessary skills to do the job. For Pam, breaking the glass ceiling wasn't her goal. Being competent, serving patients well and strengthening the hospital were her goals, and she didn't want to be the person who caused problems.

Pam's graduation in 1984 allowed her to move "downstairs."

Her style of management as one of very few women in administration was recognizably different from that of her peers. Pam balanced her competence with compassion, empathizing with those she worked with and for and she was recognized for it. In a letter from Steven Morgan, an assistant administrator, she was told: "Your experience has always been ... beneficial to me, and with a group of fairly young co-workers...you have always exhibited to me the rather unusual talents of being personally concerned about our patients both in a singular sense as well as the broader prospective that we must have to operate this institution successfully."

Despite her move downstairs, Pam wasn't ready to put away her white nursing cap either, continuing to serve as the president of the New Mexico Society for Nursing Service Administrators.

As a lead administrator over outpatient services and ambulatory clinics, Pam was highly visible in the hospital. Jamie Silva-Steele has never forgotten the first department heads meeting she attended under Pam in the 1980s. She reminisced, "I was impressed with how smart and articulate she was. She never used notes. She was just a walking encyclopedia with things that were going on in the hospital. And she was a woman and a successful leader. I thought, 'Maybe I can do that someday.'"

Pam running a meeting at the hospital.

At that time, Jamie was invested in a job she loved as the charge nurse in a pediatric unit. Pam noticed the quality of her work and leadership in her department and learned more about her background. When she discovered that Jamie had a business degree, she called her into her office and told her in her warm, direct way, "You need to be in management." Jamie decided to take Pam's encouragement and applied for a new job running two ambulatory clinics. From there she began moving up the administrative ladder with Pam as her mentor.

Jamie recalled, "Pam was so great at mentorship. I had lots of bosses before and after her but few that take time to listen and help you in your role. She was very much a visible leader. I learned that you need to be present in the places where people are because that's how you see how you can guide or remove barriers. She would physically be present in clinics and when she saw great things happening, she wrote a note and made it a big deal. She made it an environment where you want to work your hardest." Jamie continued working with UNM Hospitals and is now the president and CEO of UNM Sandoval Regional Medical Center.

FAMILY

While working as rising star in administration at UNM hospital, Pam was also learning how to negotiate being a wife and mother at home. The relationship between Pam and Jerry and Jerry's ex-wife, Jane, was tense but they worked to keep it peaceful. Pam never became comfortable calling herself the girls' mother because their mother was still living, but she invested like a mother in their lives, helping with homework, decorating their rooms, and attending special events.

Maureen Boshier recalled: "Pam loved her family. Number one in her life was her husband and girls. Jerry was perfect for her. He was patient and loving. She always thought of them first and did not accept jobs or responsibilities that would take her away from family."

One way she kept a work/life balance was through celebrations. Pam made Christmas the highlight of the year. Each holiday season, she and Jerry invited friends and acquaintances who didn't have other family to join them for Christmas Eve. Pam decorated and filled a stocking for every person attending and heaped wrapped presents for everyone around the tree. To top off the celebration, she and Jerry also cooked their favorite homemade meal of the year. Together in the kitchen they made a huge prime rib dinner, complete with coleslaw, macaroni salad, and potatoes. Jerry added a huge pot of chile from Vigil family recipes. They rounded out the meal with a feast of pies and different kinds of bread. They relished the time they spent together eating, trading stories, and laughing with guests. After dinner Pam would drink Bailey's and coffee as she relaxed with guests.

Jennifer, Pam, Jacqueline, and Jerry at Christmas.

Another highlight of family life was a yearly road trip to Cheboygan. Pam lived for her yearly fix of Michigan trees, water, and friends, and enthusiastically planned each route around amusement parks, stopping at a new one each time to try out the rollercoasters. The higher and faster they were, the better Pam and the girls liked them. Jerry loved the amusement park food and seeing the family enjoy themselves, but he didn't share their love of fast rides. He waited on the ground, holding purses and drinks.

Pam with childhood friends, Sheryl, Mary Lou, and Majel.

In Michigan, Pam shared the Galbraith family history with Jerry and the girls. She also took them on a grand tour of all her favorite sights, including the Mackinaw Bridge, the lighthouse in Cheboygan, and Lake Huron. She connected with old friends at class reunions, getting drinks around town while they reminisced. Jerry loved attending every reunion with her and was eventually made an honorary member of her class.

PROMOTION

Pam finished her Master in Business Administration from the University of Phoenix in 1987. In a leadership training program, Pam took the famed Meyers-Briggs survey and discovered that she had the rare ENTP personality type: extroverted, intuitive, thinking and perceptive. Almost everyone who worked closely with her agreed that she was an outstanding combination of bold, kind, caring leadership.

Once she had her master's degree, Bill Johnson was able to promote her and in 1988, Pam was made an assistant administrator for the hospital. Now in charge of medical services, managing geriatrics and cancer programs, she also oversaw clinical services in internal medicine, neurology, psychiatry, and dermatology. In a letter to Pam, Bill commended her for "a promotion well deserved!" Another letter mentioned that her "accomplishments are wonderful examples of what can be done when individuals take special interest and make extraordinary efforts."

Continuing to serve the community by driving the visibility of the hospital, Pam worked as UNM Hospital liaison to the annual Albuquerque Health Fair, taught classes and assisted clinical students through the UNM School of Medicine.

In the 1980s, more women began moving into administration, including Pam's friend, Maureen Boshier, who joined the hospital leadership team in 1988 as the senior administrator for surgical services. Their paths didn't cross often, but as friends of many years, they enjoyed taking time to go out together off the clock. Maureen and Pam also met up at meetings of the New Mexico Society for Nursing Service Administrators.

"She was very intelligent and a great strategist," Maureen recalled. "She was able to create well-founded strategies for how to accomplish things. She was very smart and didn't suffer fools gladly. She was often critical of other people's decisions and she wasn't easy to get along with all the time. But whatever Pam did, she was a true advocate in the healthcare field, for patients and consumers…truly for whomever she served."

As an advocate, Pam had an open-door policy, unusual at that time. She was always available to talk, guide, and help. She was also constantly on the go. With the large, round glasses of the 1980s and short greying hair, she now wore a variety of work suits with skirts and jackets that she loved to combine with matching purses and shoes. She had now magically become the executive wearing a suit, and she exerted a considerable amount of charisma and influence.

Pam, P.J. Woods, and Amy Boule,
three of the first female administrators at the hospital.

FRENEMIES

While Pam could get a room of people moving one way, she had a strong personality that clashed at times with other strong personalities. When she met Amy Boule, sparks flew.

Amy was a hospital administrator for the professional and support services, or, in her words, "everything that everyone complains about." She and Pam had first encountered one another in the early '80s when Amy still worked at the hospital laboratory. Their encounters were not warm and became icy once Amy was promoted into administration.

Confrontational whenever they met, only a common issue could unite them. Each year, UNM Hospital sent its management to Ghost Ranch in Abiquiu to plan for the upcoming fiscal year, as well as to rest and unify through team building exercises. Administrators were divided into teams, and Pam and Amy were placed together on the green team. The theme for the team building exercises was creative cheating. Pam and Amy quickly realized that while their group was not very creative or original, they could cheat. They decided that cheating would make them creative.

Team building at Ghost Ranch in Abiquiu.

The team prepared to compete in the required games. As the strongest personalities, Pam and Amy were placed in charge of their team. They decided to creatively cheat by making themselves the winners of every category. Pam and Amy were given the job of announcing all of the winners for each category. "All the scores were posted where everyone could see them," Amy reminisced. "So, as we announced the winners of each category, we reminded everyone that the theme was creative cheating and even though we hadn't won anything, we gave all the awards to ourselves."

The green team "won," but what they had thought to be a clever strategy angered the entire staff and gained them a major reprimand by their leadership. They were rebuked and told they had ruined the Ghost Ranch experience. They were also asked to apologize to everyone, which they did, singing the song "I'm Sorry" by Brenda Lee. "We were apologetic but unrepentant," Amy laughed. "And after that we decided we could get together."

Their friendship quickly grew into what Amy described as a Thelma and Louise relationship. They frequently grabbed a beer after work, talking about kids and grandkids. Back at work and unified, they channeled that recognition for a job well done by creating People's Choice awards to recognize the hospital staff members who did a great job. These awards lasted several years, spearheaded by Pam and Amy.

Maureen Boshier, Amy Boule, and Pam.

UNM administrative staff and Pam at a UNM Hospital picnic.

TRANSITION

For about 10 years Pam and Jerry had shared custody of Jerry's youngest daughter, Jennifer, who stayed with them on weekends. Relations with Jerry's ex-wife Jane were strained, and they avoided contact with her to maintain peace in the family.

At Thanksgiving in 1987, Jacqueline had gone to spend time with her mom. Her mom told her that she was not feeling well and asked Jacqueline to make the meal. Jacqueline mentioned to Pam and Jerry that her mom didn't seem well. A few months later, Pam and Jerry went to Jennifer's school to see her receive an award from the National Honors Society. At the ceremony they encountered Jerry's ex-wife and were shocked at her condition. She was gaunt yet bloated.

Realizing she desperately needed medical care, Pam checked her into UNM Hospital the next day. The doctors discovered that she had an abdominal tumor and operated immediately. The tumor had grown to 17 pounds and her prognosis wasn't good. After the surgery she went home, where she lived for a few more months, racked by fear. Jennifer helped take care of her mom before and after school. She increasingly disliked coming home from school because she was afraid she would find her mom dead. Eventually Jane was put in hospice care.

Pam was at her best when someone was in need and made herself constantly available to Jane. She was especially fearful at night and would call Pam. Warmly compassionate, Pam would tell her funny stories and play her songs on the harmonica. They talked for hours. When she passed away, Jennifer moved in with Jerry and Pam.

For Jennifer, despite being full of grief for her mom, the transition was not as challenging as it could have been, coming as it did in her freshman year of high school. She was also moving to a familiar home. She transitioned easily with the support of her sister, who moved home from college to be with her.

Jerry, Jacqueline, Jennifer and Pam on a trip to Scotland.

HIV

UNM Hospital was not only a hospital for Albuquerque; it was a hospital for the state of New Mexico. Through strategic partnerships with small clinics throughout the state, the hospital was mobilized to give care to patients in rural areas. These partnerships were vital when waves of need crossed the state. In the 1970s, the plague, hantavirus, and tuberculosis were three major killers in New Mexico's rural areas.

A new disease created fresh challenges in the 1980s: HIV. After it was first discovered, it began moving quickly and little was understood about how it spread. Fearful of contracting it personally, many hospitals and clinics had staff unwilling to work with patients who had contracted it. Pam and other doctors and nurses remained willing to treat HIV patients, making UNM Hospital one of the only options for treatment in New Mexico. As HIV spread across the state, the extreme distances combined with clinic doctors and nurses refusing HIV patients became a huge issue.

By the early 1990s, more was understood about the disease and new safety standards, including wearing face masks and latex gloves to serve patients, helped protect healthcare professionals. New medical treatments helped create positive outcomes in patients with consistent medical care. However, HIV was taking a heavy toll in remote areas of New Mexico. Pam longed to change that.

Pam giving a presentation.

New governmental funding, the Ryan White grant, was signed into law in 1990. The grant was one of the first federal governmental grants focused on caring for marginalized and remote people who contracted HIV. UNM Hospital was the perfect candidate and in prime position to care for patients in a state whose communities were separated by massive stretches of highway.

Dixon Duval managed ambulatory services at UNM Hospital. When Pam applied for and received the Ryan White grant for the hospital, she knew that the small clinics were unlikely to feel more willing to treat HIV patients unless there was a direct relationship. Together with Dixon, she began driving to small primary care clinics in remote corners of the state to try to persuade rural physicians to see HIV-positive patients.

Dixon recalled, "She was particularly good at building relationships in small towns. It seemed like she could pick out someone and develop a good working relationship." That talent tied back to her small-town upbringing. Pam was able to convince those rural physicians that they were key in increasing positive outcomes for HIV patients. According to Dixon, "Pam was always able to get the resources we needed." Pam and Dixon spent eight years working under the grant, ensuring that HIV-positive patients across New Mexico had access to high-quality care.

20 MAGICAL YEARS

By 1992, Pam had spent 20 years in New Mexico and at UNM Hospital. Jacqueline and Jennifer were both in college now, with Jacqueline pursuing her master's and Jennifer becoming a veterinarian. The open-door policy held by Pam extended to the girls' friends. One such friend, Ildikó Oravecz, lived with Jacqueline for a summer while she was in college and shared her thoughts on Pam. "I had never met anyone like her. In my mind I knew, 'This is a high-powered businesswoman.' She was a force of nature. You felt her presence. She was never still."

Pam and Chris Sykes with other UNM
administrators on a team-building rafting trip.

SAVING SANTA ROSA

Pam reveled in the "magical" opportunities given to her through the growth and development of UNM Hospital, and a new opportunity was about to come her way.

In 1993, Dr. Charles Young decided to leave his role running a hospital in Santa Rosa, and he took what he could with him. For two years he had been the only physician in a 200-mile area and had leased the hospital through his for-profit corporation. Frustrated that he was unable to get a backup physician, and accused of Medicaid fraud, he loaded beds, sheets, toilet seats, lightbulbs and medical files into a hospital trailer and left town in the middle of the night. He also left an entire region without a hospital.

A hospital closing in Santa Rosa was a critical emergency both locally and nationally because of its location on I-40 between Tucumcari and Albuquerque. If this hospital closed, another 150 miles would be added to the commute to a hospital, and people could die before receiving care. Additionally, usually within six months of a rural hospital closure most doctors' offices in the area close as well, creating an additional vacuum in patient care.

The Guadalupe County Commission, knowing they needed to resurrect the hospital, asked then-Governor Bruce King for help. He asked UNM Hospital to step in and help. After talking to the governor, Bill Johnson sent Pam to meet with Gino Lujan, a county officer, to evaluate the need. UNM Hospital wasn't willing to send staff and management, so Pam and her co-workers from the hospital began to travel on weekends, evenings, or through taking comp time and vacation time.

When Pam sat down with Gino Lujan at Joseph's Restaurant in Santa Rosa, they ordered beers and began to talk about what to do. They had visited the hospital and toured the dark, barren facility with flashlights. As they talked, the owner of the restaurant, Joseph Campos, listened. Gino and Pam realized that they needed three things: a good relationship with the community, money, and resources to restock the hospital.

Joseph introduced himself and told them he had the person they needed for community building — his wife. Christina Campos was a mom with three small kids. She ran the books for Joseph's restaurant and felt stir-crazy. The Campos family was already well-known in the community. She wanted more to do.

Christina met up with Pam and Gino at the hospital and took a flashlight tour. As a mother in the community with no access to medical care, she was worried. She agreed to help as a volunteer for a few months, working with the community and Pam to get a resources for the hospital.

Pam at a community meeting in Santa Rosa.
Gino Lujan is sitting in front of her.

Governor King pledged $75,000 to keep the hospital afloat until permanent funding became available. Meanwhile, Pam headed back to UNM Hospital. She went down into the basements and out to the surplus storage areas and found beds, toilet seats, lights, trays, and more. She talked to Toni Armijo in the pharmacy and Amy Boule. They found nearly expired medications, bandages and more to fill the cabinets. Gino Lujan sent stock trailers from Santa Rosa to transport the supplies, and Pam and her peers filled them up.

Christina began talking to the community, asking people and business owners for their thoughts about the hospital, their understanding of the need, and willingness to engage.

With beds back in the rooms, cabinets full of supplies, lightbulbs and toilet seats replaced, the hospital was in working order. Locally, Christina and Pam recruited a tiny staff, willing to wait for health insurance and pay in order to get the hospital re-booted. Christina recalled, "With Pam, there was never a question of *if* something could be done. She was the ultimate crisis manager. She thrived in chaos, pulling teams together, delegating, and appointing work."

Once they were ready to open, Bill connected Pam with Arthur Kaufman, M.D. (now distinguished professor of Family and Community Medicine), who worked for UNM Medical School and the office of community health. Arthur had worked extensively in rural areas of New Mexico, and after travelling to Santa Rosa understood the need well. He worked with Pam and sent medical residents out to the hospital in a rotation. "It was probably illegal, because they had no oversight," he commented. "They stabilized the hospital."

One resident Dr. Kaufman brought in was Randal Brown, an intern in his first year of residency at UNM. Randal was from Santa Rosa and had "left on purpose." Governor King had known Randal and his family from Santa Rosa, and specifically requested Dr. Kaufman send him. Randal was reluctant to return to his hometown, but Dr. Kaufman convinced him, fast-tracking his residential training to include extensive shifts in the emergency and trauma departments. At the beginning of July 1993, he arrived back in Santa Rosa as "a one-year trained resident to an essentially empty hospital." He worked 24/7 for two years as the only doctor on call.

With a minimal staff, a medical doctor and regular access to supplies, the hospital needed financial security from the community. Pam and Christina began coordinating a mill levy to provide permanent funding. Unfortunately, the community was against it. Santa Rosa residents knew a hospital was a good thing, but it was hard to say yes to a new tax in one of the poorest counties in New Mexico.

Christina came up with a brilliant idea to help the community see how financially vital the hospital would be to the community. She told Pam that they should have the staff get paid in $2 bills, and then spend them for everything. Pam and Christina worked with a local bank that agreed to allow the staff to cash their checks and receive pay in $2 bills.

The hospital's payroll was only about $28,000 for one month, but that made for 14,000 $2 bills. For a month, every staff person used only $2 bills for every single transaction. They paid rent and utilities, bought groceries and gas with $2 bills. Christina and Pam also took out ads in the local papers and on TV telling everyone to take note of the $2 bills. They even had the local news cover the $2 bill idea. Two-dollar bills filled up the cash drawers of every business and every wallet in Santa Rosa.

After a month, Christina personally went to each business and door-to-door. Tangibly seeing the economic impact of the hospital in their community, the Santa Rosa community of 3000 voted "yes" to the mill levy, creating permanent funding for the hospital.

Christina's three-months of volunteer work extended, and she stayed on at the hospital learning the administrative ropes. Christina said that she often felt out of her depth. Over countless phone calls, Pam would tell her, "You've got to be strong, kiddo. You've got this."

Pam at a community health fair in Santa Rosa,
promoting the hospital.

Ildikó recalled Pam coming home from Santa Rosa, still in her business suit, tossing a tortilla in the microwave, and sharing stories. "I think empathy is what women bring to the workforce, and she had that emotion in the workplace. It impacted me, because I perceived her as a very strong woman, and to see that emotion and to see how much she cared was very impactful because it showed me she wasn't this superwoman going into it," Ildikó recalled. "She had so much empathy and compassion about [Santa Rosa]. I remember her crying about it, she was so emotionally invested."

Saving a rural hospital wasn't all Pam did in Santa Rosa. She found someone new to mentor in Christina Campos, now the hospital administrator in Santa Rosa. "She was a bundle of energy," Christina said. "She always drank coffee and smoked. I could follow the trail of smoke to her."

Pam's mentorship style was active. Christina recalled: "She always invited me to training and meetings in Albuquerque, even though she knew I was a novice."

Pam recognized Christina's talent in administration, and tucked her under her wing, showing her how to lead and building up her confidence. Christina rose to the challenges Pam gave her. Christina remembered Pam pointing her out: "I was called to attend a meeting at UNM (run by Pam). At one point she looked at me with palpable pride and said, 'You know, six months ago, this kid didn't know anything and now listen to her.' I think that was a big moment, a very proud moment for her."

Randal Brown was largely working on his own, separate from the work Pam and Christina were doing. Pam would check in with him periodically to see what he needed; she was who Randal went to when he needed any equipment from beds and gauze to IV needles and medication. From his view, "She was a tough lady. I think she probably had a certain amount of skepticism because of my limited training background."

One of Randal's biggest obstacles was being alone. Working alone meant he had no one to consult if he needed help deciding on how to care for a patient. He could call UNM Hospital's operator, who would see if they could find him someone to talk to. At times a call back could be up to 24 hours later. Pam was concerned. "How do we support this kid in Santa Rosa?" she asked herself. Out of their talks, a hotline was created to ensure that providers had access to knowledge and skills of their peers around the state. "It was a game-changer for all rural doctors in New Mexico. What we needed as healthcare providers was to be able to get in touch with someone in every specialty who was on call." The new hotline was called PAL, which was a specific phone number connected with the hospital operator, who connected the rural doctor to an assigned person on call in every department in the hospital. If the attending doctor couldn't respond immediately, they were given 10 minutes to call back. Now Randal could get an attending physician to consult with, brainstorm, or transfer patients to within 10 minutes. PAL was one of the first telementoring programs for primary care physicians in the country, later followed by project ECHO.

In addition to PAL, Pam worked with Dr. Kaufman, to put together a permanent program through UNM called Partners in Health that rotated doctors through rural hospitals, bringing services to people who lacked medical coverage. Partners in Health put UNM Hospital and the medical school on the forefront of rural medicine, gaining UNM Hospital national recognition. It also added a program called Health Smart that changed the focus from hospital-led care to patient-led care. As part of Health Smart, UNM Hospital would run clinics at local schools and malls, allowing people to get blood pressure tests and more. Since then, they have remained consistently in the top 5 hospitals for rural health initiatives in the country.

UNM hospital administrative staff, including Pam, with former New Mexico Senator Pete Domenici.

TURNAROUND

Rescuing the hospital launched Pam into the limelight. Her work was covered by *48 Hours*, and her development of Partners in Health and Health Smart earned her the most prestigious award she had won to date: the YWCA of Albuquerque's Women on the Move award in 1993. Because of her success in Santa Rosa, President George H.W. Bush placed her on a national task force for rural medicine.

Ironically, her story getting featured *48 Hours* was problematic for Pam, who was still a speeder. When *48 Hours* covered her work in Santa Rosa, a camera shot showed her going 90 miles an hour. Shortly after it aired, the sheriff of the area, who knew Pam because he had given her countless tickets, called and asked her to come in. He lectured her on driving slowly and safely, but his warning fell on deaf ears. Pam continued to speed as she drove Santa Rosa three to four times per week, 120 miles away from her home. Pam simply liked to live her life full speed ahead.

Nancy Bannister worked as Pam's assistant for several years. When Pam advanced into administration and needed an assistant, she asked Nancy to consider the position. Nancy recalled, "In 1994 she approached me, and I basically disregarded that opportunity. After 10 years in the ER, I knew all the battles, department heads, staff, and loved my colleagues. Pam came to me again, saying she liked my energy and confidence and asked me to reconsider." Nancy was convinced to move and worked with Pam until 1999.

"Pam had enough moxie to walk without a big ax; she walked with her knowledge and logic, and that was how she made friends. She put 2 and 2 together quicker than anybody I know. It was a great expertise of hers." And it was an expertise she would continue to use.

Throughout the 1990s Pam would become what she termed the "turnaround administrator" for several other hospitals and clinics in rural areas of New Mexico, including Sierra Vista Hospital in Truth or Consequences, Hidalgo Medical Services in southern New Mexico, and a medical clinic in Mountainair. It was a role she loved, and she told Jerry that she found chaos exciting.

Because of her success in Santa Rosa, she was called on by Governor King and various senators to discuss rural health and health care delivery issues in New Mexico. UNM Hospital expanded her role, making her Administrator of Ambulatory Services and Rural & Community Outreach Programs. She was also appointed as co-chair of the UNM Health Sciences Rural Outreach Committee.

For several years she continued working nationally on rural health initiatives, later getting invited to participate in President Clinton's Rural Healthcare Forum. She even stepped up to work with the New Mexico Rural Development Response Council, where she served as board member, vice president, and president.

CANCER

Back in Albuquerque, Pam and Jerry wanted to build a new home. A new neighborhood was being built near the foothills of the Sandia Mountains, and it would be easy for Pam to drive to work from the area. As building goes, the process was not easy. Work on the house was begun in April 1994 and contracted to be complete by July. Due to mismanagement the home was nowhere near ready. Christmas was Pam's favorite holiday, and she and Jerry demanded that the builders finish by Christmas Eve, telling them that they had never not had a Christmas at home and didn't intend to begin now.

Confident that their home would be done, Jerry and Pam had sold their previous home and even moved their personal belongings into their new garage. They spent the first weeks of December in a hotel while the builders managed to complete the house. Pam triumphantly plugged in a tiny Christmas tree on Christmas Eve. They had no furniture, but they still held stripped-down festivities in the home.

Jacqueline, Jennifer, Pam, and Jerry.

Pam and Jerry loved working in the community on their days off. Jerry volunteered for the University of New Mexico Men's Golf Association. Jerry had volunteered as the president and coordinated several events including the Tucker Tournament in 1996. The event went well but he told Pam he didn't feel well during the tournament. Pam scheduled a checkup. He felt better when he rested after the tournament but decided to go to the appointment. During his exam, the doctor discovered a lesion on Jerry's prostate. He ran tests and called Jerry to tell him it seemed to be cancer. Pam was on her way to Santa Rosa when Jerry called with the news.

Terrified, Pam called her close friends Gino Lujan and his wife, Linda, crying. Although she worked in medical care, a diagnosis like cancer seemed immediately terminal and she began to imagine life without Jerry. The Lujans helped her calm down, and she turned around and headed back to Albuquerque.

Jerry went in for more testing. In front of Jerry, Pam seemed stoic, waiting for a more definite diagnosis. The doctor knew Pam and Jerry were about to go on a trip out of town, but he called them in the day before they left to tell Jerry that it was indeed cancer, and he would need surgery. Pam had always paid attention to how patients were treated, and she was furious that the doctor would tell them just before a trip. She would often cry with anger, and in that instance she did, scolding the doctor for not breaking the news more gently and not waiting until after their trip.

Jerry required immediate surgery. It was successful, and the cancer was completely gone, but he needed rest to recover.

To recover, Jerry decided to take a break from his personal insurance business to help run a flower shop with Pam's older sister, Beth Ann.

Beth Ann had moved to Albuquerque several years earlier to live closer to her children. She had always wanted to open a flower shop, and Jerry and Pam lent her money to launch it. Because of his experience with finances, Jerry took care of the books. He also made deliveries while Beth Ann created flower arrangements.

Jerry and Pam at a UNM Hospital formal event.

Pam and Beth Ann had often had a difficult relationship, partly due to the sisters' extremely different personalities. After two years, the challenges of working together came to a head.

Determined to keep peace within the family, Jerry left the floral shop and never returned. He told Pam what happened. Pam went to Beth Ann and told her that they forgave the loan, giving her the business. She also told her that Jerry would not return. Beth Ann stayed in business just a few more months before closing her shop and moving back to Cheboygan, where she opened a new floral shop under the same name.

Jerry was strong and healthy, the girls were in college, and Pam was thriving at work. Then, in 1998 Pam was diagnosed with breast cancer. The diagnosis wasn't a surprise as almost every nurse and doctor who had worked with chemotherapy in the 1970s and '80s had become ill with some kind of cancer due to their exposure to the treatment chemicals. Despite not feeling well, she shared her prognosis with very few people. She went into treatment at the cancer center at UNM, and spent six months going into the cancer center every other week in the mornings for radiation. After her treatments, she would head to her office and continue working. She didn't miss a single day of work.

Cancer helped Pam achieve one lifelong goal: stop smoking. Her Tareyton cigarettes had been a beloved but an unfortunate addiction for years. Her cancer diagnosis gave her the perfect reason to quit. In an effort to improve her health, she also gave up her favorite foods, including bacon and bagels. When Pam had her final treatment, the cancer center staff treated her to a bagel and cream cheese served with bacon on a silver platter, complete with a cloche. Delighted, Pam ate every bite.

After her treatment ended, Jerry and Pam, with characteristic generosity, took the entire staff of the cancer center to a personalized meal at the well-known Rancher's Club as a "thank-you" for their tremendous care. It was fine dining with fine friends and providers. They gave Pam her health back, which made Pam feel that magic was still a part of her story.

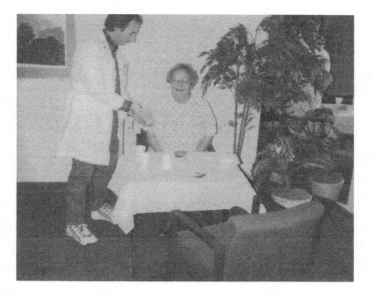

Pam finishing cancer treatment with a bagel and cream cheese.

MOVEMENT

Pam had worked under Bill Johnson as CEO for almost her entire career. When he announced his retirement, two possible candidates were considered: Pam and Steve McKernan. Pam only discussed the position with Jerry, and her closest friends never knew she had been considered for the position. She wrestled with the possibility for weeks. CEO of the hospital she loved would mean making a greater impact for healthcare in many ways, but the position would limit her ability to do other parts of the job she loved and ultimately, she removed herself from consideration.

Steve McKernan was named CEO, and under his leadership the hospital continued to operate well. Then, in late 1999, Steve asked Pam to pivot and take over as administrator of behavioral health services. Pam was shocked. She had minimal exposure to behavioral healthcare. During her nursing training in Cheboygan, she had interned at a local mental health facility and found the experience terrifying.

Pam told Steve that she was not interested in the role. She was passionate about working in the hospital. Steve, however, made it clear that moving to behavioral health was her only choice if she wanted to continue working at UNM Hospital. She unwillingly accepted and announced the change. Co-workers at the time were surprised by the move. Emails and notes of surprise and congratulations for her new position poured in. Pam told only a few close friends about her anger and suspicion that the move was punitive in some way. She definitely didn't see magic in this opportunity.

When asked, Steve recalled, "Behavioral health was a train wreck. It was not serving the community well. The clinics were backed up beyond belief, the latest and best protocols for treating mental illness were not there, and physician management wasn't contemporary." The turnaround administrator for multiple rural hospitals was a logical choice to fix all those things. The decision to move Pam also coincided with the hospital's plan to move all the behavioral health clinics under the umbrella of UNM Hospital.

Pam didn't know much about the behavioral health scene. She approached it like a rural hospital needing help. She began by going to every department and learning who worked there and what they did. She asked questions about systems and patients. She studied the clinics that fed into the hospital. She spent time in the children's psychology department, which included dorms and a school because the average stay was more than 200 days.

She saw that the clinics were backlogged, with up to a three-month wait to get in, and the structure of everything from the hospital to the clinics was extremely fragmented.

After a few months, Pam realized that she was in familiar territory, with chaos that needed to be organized. Despite beginning with no experience or interest in behavioral health, seeing the need aroused her compassion and commitment to serving everyone as well as she would want to be served herself. She threw herself completely in.

She would succeed, but the pressure of the move was hard to handle. One night in the kitchen she and Jerry were talking when she surprised him by saying, "I feel like smoking again. Do you mind?" Jerry told her she could if it would make her feel better. She began the next day.

Rodney McNease, the executive director of governmental affairs for UNM Hospitals and overseer of operational collaborations at the Psychiatric Center, met Pam in 2000 after she moved to behavioral health. He recalled her move: "There was a huge amount of transition. Pam worked to bring groups together in a way that had a unified approach on how UNM dealt with behavioral health services. One of the biggest accomplishments she had was her ability to understand how things needed to be organized and leverage things together that hadn't been before."

One problem she encountered was familiar: ego. Physicians and clinic operators wanted to be independently authoritative. This created a constantly fractured system. Pam, given carte blanche, reorganized internal systems to free up the clinics so people could get immediate care, eliminating the backlog in the clinics. She actively recruited more physicians to expand their reach. She studied standards nationwide and created standards for a better psychiatric ER. She also worked to create new channels of communication between the ER and clinics.

Another challenge in behavioral health was keeping patients healthy after treatment. Pam worked to develop new programs and protocols that created a more consistent treatment for patients, moving from an all-or-nothing approach to treatment to a gradual tapering of care. Because of her background in physical health, she had experienced firsthand the way behavioral and physical healthcare worked together. Now she was in a place to create discussions and programs to tie the two together, uncommon at the time. "These were really difficult programs to develop," Steve recalled. "Pam had very good organizational skills and a remarkable ability to empathize with others, and was unwilling to compromise her principles. She had a sincere belief that UNM Hospital was the key to taking care of the vulnerable in the community."

Her hard work paid off, and after three years, the behavioral health centers were under the auspices of UNM Hospital and running smoothly. With her reorganization, they were meeting new levels of quality care and saving lives. For Pam, once again, the bottom line was about producing the best possible outcomes for patients. She saw the need and the path forward.

Pam had long recognized a lack of community health-care programs outside of the hospital. She advocated for and helped create new programs for key issues that were crippling New Mexicans, such as programs for alcohol abuse and methadone treatment. She took her ideas on the road and began to advocate for the notion that more money spent on addiction services saved money downstream in corrections and other areas. Already connected to presidential panels, her advocacy created national awareness of this need.

Pam's move created much-needed changes for New Mexico that ushered in a new era for behavioral health. Rodney said, "The behavioral health environment in New Mexico is extraordinarily challenging. New Mexico has historically lagged behind other states, and we are on the bottom rung. Pam took a huge advocacy role with the state and other providers related to behavioral health services."

The state took notice of Pam's work, and she was asked by the governor's office to serve as a member of the Medicaid Behavioral Health Steering Committee in 2002. President George W. Bush was working with New Mexico senators on creating the New Freedom Commission on Mental Health, the first mental health commission created by a president in 25 years. He announced his hopes for the commission at a speech in Albuquerque. President Bush, who knew of Pam from her previous work with both his father and President Clinton, wrote a letter to Pam stating, "Thank you for your hospitality during my visit ... last week to talk about improving access to quality mental health care. I appreciate you sharing your thoughts."

Pam and President George W. Bush at a formal event.

From this meeting, Pam was invited to participate in a Mental Health Issues Round Table with the president. In 2003, Attorney General John Ashcroft appointed Pam to be a part of the U.S. Departments of Health and Human Services National Advisory Committee on Violence Against Women, a small committee with only 20 members.

Shortly after this appointment, she was selected to serve on the governing council of the American Hospital Association for Psychiatric and Substance Abuse Services, on which she served for three years as a member of the governing council, advising on strategies and positions as well as serving as a liaison. On taking the position she commented, "The access, financial, and regulatory issues facing New Mexico's psychiatric facilities jeopardizes our ability to meet the needs of our population. This council will give me the opportunity to promote the development of policies and programs to better serve our clients."

While much of her work focused on adult behavioral health, Pam developed a special affinity for the children's psychiatric department. The children's area was fairly well organized at the time, so her work initially only included moving it under the management of UNM Hospital. From there it went through radical changes, including increased involvement from the government and Medicaid. Her work allowed her to see the impact helping young people would have on their futures. Pam would continue to care for children's behavioral health throughout her life.

Pam was now in her 50s and had been working in healthcare for over 30 years. She had helped radically change the direction of a hospital, of rural medical care for the marginalized, and now she was helping shape medical and behavioral healthcare on a national level. Amy shared that her only concern was being forgotten when she was gone.

Her work for the women and children of New Mexico after her move to behavioral health administration earned her the Governor's Award for Outstanding New Mexico Women in 2003. In addition to winning that award, she was one of two women inducted into New Mexico Women's Hall of Fame for her service. Letters, calls and emails of congratulation came in from the president, state senators, the governor, other hospital administrators, friends and co-workers.

Pam speaking at a national healthcare event.

Already prominent in the state for medical work, she was appointed to the New Mexico Medicaid Advisory Committee, and was now able to help set Medicaid policy and determine program direction. A year later, as she continued to change the direction of UNM behavioral health services, with an appointment from the governor as a member of the Behavioral Health Planning Council.

In a few short years she had grabbed hold of a challenge she didn't like, and radically changed the direction of behavioral health in New Mexico and the nation.

30 MAGICAL YEARS

Pam didn't only keep news clippings and copies of awards and congratulations marking her rise in her field. She also kept clippings of happenings in Cheboygan, as well as personal birthday and Christmas cards. She even kept a birthday telegram from her first year of college.

Pam and Jerry's 25th anniversary celebration.

Even after spending more than 30 yers in New Mexico, Pam's year still revolved around planned relaxation in Cheboygan with close friends from childhood and her dose of green and trees. She and friends including Sheryl, Lynn, Kathy, Majel, and others would get together for meetups around the county. These times with friends were highlights in her year, satisfying her need for water and to remember her roots.

Jacqueline and Jennifer had both grown up now. Both were married and beginning families. Pam and Jerry were empty nesters, enjoying life together.

Jerry, Pam, Jacqueline and her husband Neil,
Jennifer and her husband Scott enjoying a meal in NYC
at the Tavern on the Green.

CLOSURE

In the early 2000s, the State of New Mexico's behavioral health system was overseen by the state Department of Health, which in turn used multiple agencies to provide and pay for behavioral health needs of patients on Medicaid and Medicare. Unfortunately, that system was extremely backlogged and payments were critically delayed. In 2005, New Mexico contracted ValueOptions to consolidate the state's 17 behavioral health organizations under one organization, with the hopes of providing a better level of care and speeding up claim payments. Because of Pam's stature and visibility, she was asked to consider working as CEO for ValueOptions in New Mexico.

UNM's behavioral health system had been vastly improved but despite her remarkable success, Pam was still not happy working for Steve. She was ready for something new and immediately said yes.

She signed a four-year contract as CEO of ValueOptions for New Mexico, with the understanding that she would be managing nearly $1 billion worth of funds over that period. She turned in her letter of resignation to Steve McKernan.

She wrote, "I want to thank you for giving me the assignment, although I took it with reluctance, to learn about the mental health field. If you had not done so, I would not have been able to take advantage of this new adventure. I wish you much success, and please know that I will be helpful to this institution in any way I can."

With that, surprising her friends and co-workers, Pam retired from UNM Hospital after 33 years of exemplary service. UNM Hospital wrote: "In our organization, Pam is known for her mentorship of rising stars, her advocacy for her areas of responsibility, her comfortable rapport with legislators, her mischievous sense of humor, her quick grasp of issues, her ability to do multiple things at the same time, and her passion for the mission of UNM Hospitals."

She left with a shower of emails and cards congratulating her and thanking her for her kindness and help throughout the years. Pam's co-workers held a banquet for her. For their perpetually fun-loving friend, they bookended the traditional buffet fare with plates towering with stacks of bacon, Pam's favorite.

Pam's retirement buffet, complete with stacks of bacon on each end.

When Pam moved to ValueOptions, she was launching a completely new initiative with no infrastructure – by now, familiar territory for her. She began her prestigious new role with only a company cell phone and a car. Building from the ground up, she began by renting offices and finding staff to fill them, both in Albuquerque and other crucial cities in New Mexico. She invited some key co-workers from UNM to join her, including Nancy Bannister. One of Nancy's first assignments was creating a computer program that showed where money to pay providers would come from. After six months, she had a running system that "braided" all of the funding together, allocating monies and services to providers as easily as possible.

Pam's headshot for work.

Once she established offices in Santa Fe, Las Cruces, and Roswell, Pam spent her time traveling and training staff to use the new program. They then trained providers and others to bill and code for proper compensation. Within a few months, she was able to take care of the backlog of payments, and with the new computer system, keep it from happening again.

New Mexico is the fifth largest state, and the sixth most sparsely populated in the country. With so much space, distance is measured in time, not miles. Santa Fe was an hour drive from Albuquerque, and Las Cruces was three hours. Pam was given use a plane, which saved hours of driving time and speeding tickets for her. It also allowed her to come home most nights.

Pam's ethical approach to healthcare and outstanding results brought her more accolades. She was recognized in ABQ the Magazine in 2006. She was also selected as a Woman of Influence in 2006 by NM Business Weekly. Business Weekly Power Book listed Pam as a 2007 Power Broker, calling her "NM's Matron of Mental Health."

NM First Lady Barbara Richardson
and Rebecca Vigil-Jiron, presenting Pam with the Governor's
Award for Outstanding New Mexico Women
and inducting her into the New Mexico Women's Hall of Fame.

Her outstanding success, surprisingly, was not appreciated by ValueOptions. Working with the backdrop of the perpetual poverty faced by many New Mexicans, Pam felt her role was to make sure ValueOptions did the job that the state of New Mexico hired them to do: allocate money and care for behavioral health services. Unfortunately, leadership at ValueOptions felt her first priority was to help the company earn money for the stockholders.

Shortly after Pam began, Barbara Hill, was hired as CEO of ValueOptions in Virginia. Soon after she assumed the role, she met with Pam and made it clear that she felt Pam was doing a thorough job. Over the next year, however, Barbara's approval for her sank as she began to take exception to some of Pam's choices. She began pressuring Pam, telling her that she was taking money from the company by not putting shareholders first. Pam disagreed. Tensions between the two grew, until they came to a head over a multi-million-dollar New Mexico state account that had not yet been awarded. Barbara demanded that Pam claim the money for ValueOptions. Pam refused, stating that the contractual money for ValueOptions had been satisfied, and the account was not part of the awarded money.

This went against the corporate culture of ValueOptions, and the leadership felt Pam had misplaced her priorities. In October 2007, Pam and Jerry were on vacation. She was asked if she would consider leaving early to attend a corporate meeting in Virginia. Pam thought the timing was strange but had no qualms in attending. As soon as she arrived, she was told that she was being fired. They stripped her of her car, keys, and every document pertaining to ValueOptions. She was even told to hand over her phone, but she asked to keep it so she could call her husband. She called Jerry, physically shaking. "They fired me," she told him, in shock. When she returned home, she attempted to go to her office, only to find that ValueOptions had changed all the locks. She was only allowed to enter her office with a security escort. It was the most painful and humiliating experience of her career.

She and Jerry hired an attorney. ValueOptions was determined to have been in breach of contract in firing her. She was compensated and publicly the company wrote her a letter, congratulating her on her "retirement." Emails and cards from friends and colleagues were sent, expressing surprise at her retirement and thanking her for her hard work.

Pam never exposed the event publicly or privately. When asked about her retirement, she stated, "I am proud to have served the state, the people of New Mexico and behavioral healthcare recipients as together we have helped improve the overall behavioral healthcare delivery system, maximized the use of existing funds and created better access to appropriate care. I leave with the pleasure and satisfaction of knowing that we have been able to play a role in reinventing the system in New Mexico and as a result improve the lives of so many people in need of services."

She also stated that she was ready to retire and spend time with her family, especially her grandkids.

BURNOUT

After being fired from ValueOptions, Pam decided to officially retire. She felt angry, humiliated and frustrated. She needed time off. She and Jerry spent time together. She took vacations and spent time with friends. She rested.

Pam swimming with her granddaughter Jaden.

Jacqueline and Jennifer were both married now. Jacqueline had three young daughters, while Jennifer had begun a veterinarian clinic. She now had two young daughters. Pam was ready to spend time with her grandchildren. "She would hold her grandkids and talk to them and just be silly," Jacqueline recalled. She was incredibly generous and loved getting gifts for her grandkids and spending time with them.

And after decades of mentoring others in leadership, she now had time to mentor Jacqueline and Jennifer. Jennifer recalled coming to Pam for advice about her veterinary clinic: "She would sit and listen, not interrupting. And then she would say, 'Here's what I would do.' And it was good, sound advice."

During her retirement, Jerry got a call from his friend Emory Chavez from Acoma Pueblo. Jerry and Emory played golf together regularly and he and his wife, Ruth, were friends with the entire family. Emory had called to tell Jerry he was in town and checking into a Lovelace hospital with a small ailment. Jerry and Pam immediately went to check in on him. His aliment was nominal, and he expected to go home in a couple of days.

Due to hospital errors, he got bedsores and contracted MRSA, which became a flesh-eating bacterium during his stay. Pam and Jerry began to visit more and Pam started keeping detailed documentation of the entire case. He died from the bacteria, leaving his wife with no retirement benefits. Because she had watched the entire case unfold, Pam felt that his death was due to a lack of proper recognition and early care from the hospital.

Pam told Ruth she needed to file a malpractice suit against the hospital and offered to help. Pam found an attorney who specialized in medical malpractice and worked with them to put the case together. The process took five years, and Pam helped prepare the malpractice suit, testifying as the expert witness. She won a large financial judgment for Ruth, allowing her to live in her retirement comfortably.

LFC

Pam was content, but her retirement didn't last long. Eight months in, Charles Sallee and David Abbey called her. They worked for the Legislative Finance Committee in Santa Fe. The LFC was a compliance evaluation department in the state government that worked to make sure tax money was being used as it was allocated.

Charles had met Pam when she ran ValueOptions because her money was allocated by the state for Medicaid and Medicare. Charles' work had included evaluating how well ValueOptions was working in correcting problems, such as providers not getting paid in a timely manner. "Pam was very cordial and pretty experienced," he said. He knew she would be a valuable asset to the committee.

Around the time Pam left ValueOptions, the LFC began to shift from compliance evaluation to impact evaluation. This meant hiring new staff. Charles asked Pam to bring her relationships and expertise into the LFC and begin helping the state of New Mexico by evaluating the impact of medical care.

After talking with Jerry, Pam agreed to work for the LFC part-time, no more than 19 hours per week.

The LFC was staffed by very young people, many of whom hoped to branch out into politics in other ways. It was thought of as a incubator of sorts to get experience and a foot in the political door.

Pam, Jerry, the girls and their husbands and grandchildren.

Pam's main motivation for working when she didn't have to was the same principle that guided her each step of her career so far: making things better for those who needed it most. Charles gave Pam projects he knew she would be passionate about and experienced in. The LFC mixed site visits with frontline staff. They would bring together qualitative and quantitative data, looking for benchmarks to see how New

Mexico was doing in various areas. It was perfect for Pam, who had already spent years traveling around New Mexico, visiting the front lines of medical facilities, behavioral health facilities and more. The pay was low for someone with Pam's status, but she saw that she could make an impact on health outcomes, and it was worth it. She also saw that the work would be low stress.

She began her work by focusing on nursing home regulation. She traveled around the state to look into nursing homes to see the level of care being given and how funds were being managed. Nathan Eckberg, a program evaluator for the LFC, came under Pam's mentorship when he began at working for the committee. One project he worked on with her was on aging and long-term services in the state.

He also worked with her on evaluating health facilities. "When we were travelling, everyone knew her. You could see the instant legitimacy and respect she brought to projects. People knew who she was and that she knew what she was talking about."

Pam also continued her advocacy and work with the behavioral health systems in New Mexico. Because of her prominence, she was able to arrange meetings with CEOs of companies who were usually unavailable to the LFC. She also led a team to find out what was driving costs for costs in mental health systems. "Her report began having a major impact on the system when we began putting in her recommendations."

Although she was hired to work part-time, Pam jumped all in, working 80-plus hours per week. She refused to be paid more, saying excellence was its own reward. Meanwhile, just one year after she left ValueOptions, it lost its contract with New Mexico.

Pam was in her 60s now, with mild COPD from years of smoking. She told Jerry that the daily drive to Santa Fe was beginning to exhaust her, but she wouldn't give it up. Jerry noticed that she wasn't eating well and had dropped several clothing sizes. He began sending her to work with peanut butter and jelly sandwiches in a brown bag.

For Pam, working at the LFC was relaxing and fulfilling. As she put it, this role was "the most fun she ever had." Many of the people working there were very young, just beginning their careers. She was a double-retiree who had loved her career. She had nothing to prove and no ambition other than to continue to help. Along with her expertise in the area of healthcare, she began mentoring the young women and men around her.

Pam during her LFC years at Gino Lujan's son's wedding with Jerry.

Charles recalls, "She was, though technically I was her supervisor, a mentor to me. She would come in my office and say, 'I was thinking about this or that. She would flag things for me. I would talk through strategies with her, and she would give me feedback."

Nathan always began his day by stopping in her office. She would give him half of the peanut butter and jelly sandwich while they talked. He would also run ideas past her, ask for help and advice. "She was so humble that you would never think she had lived the life that she did. She believed in true mentorship; not just about on the job stuff but life-mentorship. She was always talking about her life and experiences in ways she thought would shepherd us along." Nathan attributes his successes to her mentorship. "She would fight for us and be an advocate in every situation."

Jon Courtney, now the deputy director at the LFC, began working at the committee in 2011. Pam was working as an evaluator with an office on the second floor of the capitol building in Santa Fe, colloquially called the Roundhouse. New hires to the LFC were put in one of four cubicles to be trained. Pam would take them under her wing, show them the methodology of the department and give them an introduction to the informal workings of the LFC—people's personalities, how to be heard, how to get a point across in context. Jon recalls that she was a huge help to on-boarding people.

She not only trained him, but "When I moved to a manager role she made my job easier. She had her finger on the pulse of the office. For five to six years she was a mentor. I learned a lot from her in dealing with office politics and office problems. She would give really great, honest advice in such a way I knew it was serious. And she was really funny. She could lighten up a serious situation pretty quickly."

Despite her incredible expertise, she didn't have much computer savvy. Spreadsheet programs were a mystery to her, and she preferred to write notes in small spiral notebooks. Analysis was a new field to her as well. Charles got her help for spreadsheets and analysis.

Pam spent eight years at the LFC, and even recruited other friends to work there. Her knack for developing solutions and gaining trust allowed her to succeed and get things moving when others couldn't. And Pam was passionate about her "kids" – an affectionate nickname for all the young staff she worked with. She would protect, help, and defend them to anyone.

Jon recalled a legendary day when an LFC report had been presented and, fearing losing funding, a member of the legislature was very harsh with the presenters. Pam caught the senator as they left the hearing room and gave them what the others termed "a talking to." Jon recalled, "She had the expertise and respect to do something like that and be heard."

Always humble, she realized that her honesty could come with repercussions and spent the next few days slinking around her office, waiting to be fired. She wasn't, and continued working at the LFC.

Jerry and the girls loved hearing about her kids at the LFC. They bought her a Keurig so she could share coffee with them. She always kept it stocked along with Twizzlers and other snacks in her office. As each person came in to her office to talk, she would brew coffee and offer snacks. She worked as a de-facto staff nurse, caring for headaches, wounds, and even serious health issues, such as treating a senator who collapsed with a heart attack. At home she told Jerry that her co-workers were rising stars, and while they were the youngest people she had ever worked with, they were the brightest.

Charles recalled that "she had a good ability to connect and get information that resonated with a hard-hitting report." And because she went to the front lines to get her information, her reports were hard to argue with, especially when they came with the support of legislators in far-flung areas of the state.

Pam rose to the level of Program Evaluator III (the highest level possible). In 2014, the NM LFC was awarded the Excellence in Research Methods, only given to three offices across the country. And in 2015, her office received the Excellence in Evaluation Award, recognizing the sole office in the nation determined to have contributed the most to the field of legislative program evaluation for the four-year period of 2012-2015.

Jerry was committed to Pam and her hard work, but with her 80-hour work week, he missed her. Jacqueline and Jennifer and her grandkids missed her too.

Jerry could see that Pam was exhausted. She had lost even more weight and clothing sizes. She had had several near accidents on the long drive to and from Santa Fe and been struck in traffic for hours. The drive began taking such a toll on her that Jerry began driving her to work, staying to play golf, and then driving her home. He asked her to consider retiring for good.

Pam agreed that it was time to step down. She planned to retire from the LFC and volunteer for the police department in Albuquerque, where she wouldn't have a long drive. She told Charles, who was disappointed, but understood. On April 8, 2016, the Friday before her final day of work at the LFC, Pam announced her retirement to the rest of the staff. She was going to leave a hole in the organization. The staff began planning a retirement party for the next week complete with an award, a proclamation recognizing her for the myriad of accomplishments she had championed for the state.

PERFECT CIRCLE

That afternoon Pam drove home from Santa Fe after announcing her retirement. She hadn't been feeling good and was glad she wouldn't have the long drive anymore. At home she put on her favorite T-shirt from the green team event at Ghost Ranch, went to her office and called her sister for a brief chat. Still not feeling well, she didn't each much dinner. She told Jerry that her back hurt, so he tried to massage it for her, but that hurt more. She had a headache and laid down on the couch with a cold compress.

Gradually she felt more and more pain in her back. Jerry offered to take her to the ER but she refused, knowing the UNM Hospital ER on a Friday night was full and she would be more comfortable at home. Around midnight she told Jerry to go to bed. He told her he would stay with her and spent the night replacing the cold compresses and trying to make her comfortable. She had had sleepless, uncomfortable nights before, and Jerry would always stay up with her to help.

Usually Pam would feel better in the morning, but this time Jerry could tell she was feeling much worse. He decided to call an ambulance. Pam was non-responsive by the time the EMTs arrived. They immediately loaded her into the ambulance and headed for UNM Hospital's ER. Jerry called his daughters as he followed the ambulance, and they rushed to meet him at the ER.

Jacqueline met him, and as they waited in a family room next to the ER, the doctor addressed them. They expected to see Pam, a lifelong fighter with boundless energy, becoming stable. Instead, they were told: "There was nothing we could do. She just had a little bit of pulse and we lost her." Shocked, Jerry and his daughters went to her room and found Pam lying on the bed. Jerry held her hand. They sat with Pam for a while. When they left to go home, a thick fog had settled over the hospital.

Later Jerry said that he was struck that Pam finished her life in the ER at UNM Hospital, the place where 44 years earlier, her career in New Mexico began. It was a perfect circle.

Jerry was overcome with grief. Instead of planning retirement, he was planning a funeral. His daughters planned a celebration of life for Pam at the Anderson-Abruzzo Albuquerque International Balloon Museum. They called every number in Pam's phone to let friends, family, and colleagues know. Shock resonated through the healthcare world and the LFC.

Jon Courtney had just finished writing a proclamation for her retirement. Now it would be a remembrance for her death. Her co-workers at the LFC were stunned. They were already struggling to imagine working without her, but they took solace in the fact that they could still call her. Now she was completely gone. The entire LFC reeled. The celebration became a remembrance ceremony for Pam, attended by her entire family. The LFC presented a plaque for her achievements to the family. Then Jerry and his daughters cleaned out her desk.

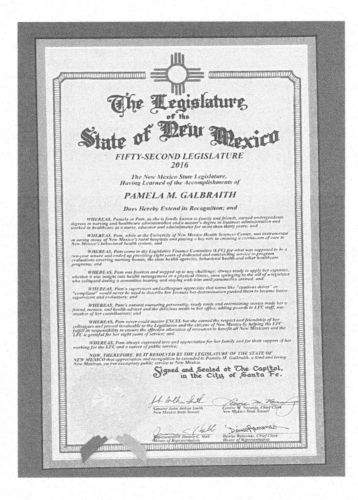

Pam's family received her proclamation posthumously on the Friday she was to retire.

Jon Courtney had just finished writing a proclamation for her retirement. Now it would be a remembrance for her death. Her co-workers at the LFC were stunned. They were already struggling to imagine working without her, but they took solace in the fact that they could still call her. Now she was completely gone. The entire LFC reeled. The celebration became a remembrance ceremony for Pam, attended by her entire family. The LFC presented a plaque for her achievements to the family. Then Jerry and his daughters cleaned out her desk.

Her celebration of life was attended by hundreds of friends, colleagues, and mentees. They took turns sharing stories and memories. They wrote notes on tiny notecards provided by the family, remembering her impact on their lives. Many attendees were unaware of her tremendous accomplishments because Pam was humble and focused on the present. What they did know was that Pam was a woman who made things happen. She was a miracle worker inside an industry and a state desperate for miracles. Pam's magical life would never be forgotten.

The End

EPILOGUE

Pam's family continues honoring her name in many ways through the Pamela Galbraith Foundation. Donations include an annual scholarship for Cheboygan High School seniors who are going to pursue secondary education in medical fields. The foundation has added another scholarship fund to the North Central Michigan College for Nursing, the college where the magic began when Pam received her nursing degree. The Grief Center for Hope and Healing in Albuquerque has a snack bar dedicated to Pam called "Pam's Place." The Grief Center also has a room for young children sponsored by the foundation. Regular financial donations are made to UNM Children's Behavioral Health and ER. Finally, Jerry keeps "Pam's Snack Shack" stocked with treats for her colleagues at the LFC.

Pam's Snack Shack at the LFC in Santa Fe.
Jerry still keeps it stocked.

"Bunches and bunches."

"Me too!"